The Wis

A Collection of Poems

by

Gillian Holland

ACKNOWLEDGEMENTS

To my Dad, long since in Spirit, who inspired this work from the 'other side of life'. And to my Ancestors.

Big thank you to my husband for believing in me, and to my family for their love and encouragement.

The Wisdom Tree Women, Daphne, Louise and Gwen, what a group of inspirational women!

To Sue Williams, who invited me to write a chapter in one of her inspirational Believe books, and who is still supporting my dreams.

To Cynthia, where would I be without our natter? What a difference talking ideas through can make.

A special mention for the Natural World, and the open countryside where I took my walks: you've taught me so much about me about healing, and how important it is to embrace change, and wide open transformative spaces.

'Eventually, my eyes were opened

and I really understood nature.

I learned to love at the same time.'

Claude Monet

THE POEMS

- Melting Pot
- Dark Dusty Boxes
- Sweet Mother
- Conversations with the Breeze
- The Ah-ha Moment
- Remembrance Day
- Tables
- Words
- Light of Hope
- A Call to Life
- Autumn's Deep Yawning
- Autumn's Rich Palette
- Tending the Earth
- Walk in the Forest
- Rainbow Bridge
- The Key to Life
- The Alchemist
- Roar
- Cauldron
- I am that I am
- On Pain and Perception

Introduction

Gillian's poetry chronicles her journey through 2020 Pandemic Lockdown, and the inspiration she drew from her daily walks in nature, as life as we knew it skidded to an abrupt halt.

This space, unlike anything else we'd known in living memory, plunged us all into complete turmoil . Inevitably, loss of life, liberty and livelihood threw up long forgotten memories also needing closure, as we grieved for what was.

Gillian was no exception, having not only lost her father as a four year old, but subsequently suffering abuse.

During this period, she crafted a poem each day: each piece weaving a connective thread between past and present experience, an opportunity to look at the current emergency, and past circumstance through a lens of infinite possibility rather than boundless loss.

Her words are intended as a celebration of our Spirit

to rise above trauma and emotions, using Nature's awesome transformational power to inspire and heal.

Each poem begins with the same words, 'Looking back over my shoulder, I can see clearly now', symbolising another poetic insight gained from her reflection.
Enjoy

The inspirational quotes

The short inspirational quotes, on the left hand pages are intended as heart openers, or an opportunity to move on as you reflect on your own lives in the tranquillity of the natural world.

Reflections, meditation and visualisation

Sitting outside in nature can be both revitalising and relaxing. It's a wonderful way to dust the cobwebs, especially if you're feeling sluggish.

Everything has its natural rhythm, including us. But sometimes we get stuck, unable to achieve closure or wholeheartedly embrace a bright new beginning. The mere act of walking, coupled with reflection in a natural environment, can help us release and come to terms with previously blocked emotions.

(To get the idea, watch the way the elements rise and fall especially the breeze or waves lapping against the seashore.)

Take this pamphlet, together with your journal out into your favourite place in nature to reflect on your own Lockdown experience. Allow it to fall open on a page of its own accord. You might be surprised at the recollections which resurface.

Try the meditation below.

Meditation

- Find a quiet place somewhere out in the natural world.
- (Alternatively, visualise this meditation in the comfort of your own home. Have poetry pamphlet, notebook and pen to hand.)
- Gillian's favourite spot is with her back against an ancient oak tree. You could, however, go for a stream or river bank, but somewhere that's safe and secluded.
- Snuggle into your chosen spot, feet outstretched, or flat on the floor, back firmly supported.
- Drink in your surroundings, feeling the breeze caressing your cheek, or rustling through the trees. Notice the way it rises, gathering momentum before falling back in to Silence.
- Then become aware of the rise and fall of your breath. Just observe without trying to alter its natural rhythm, the in breath and then the out breath.
- As you continue to observe, notice how quite naturally the breath drops into your belly. As you breathe in, your belly begins to lift; and as you breathe out, your belly lowers back towards the spine. All without effort. Your body is breathing you.
- As you observe your body's natural rhythms, feel the Sun's gentle warmth on your shoulders, and if you're lucky enough to be by water, experience

the impact its sound has on you, as you become Immersed and at one with the world about you.

- Pick up your booklet, allow it to fall open as it will.
- Reflect on your chosen page.
- See what naturally comes to mind, before jotting any thoughts down.
- Don't push, stay open. Maintain a natural relaxed breath throughout
- Observe
- It may be that your inspiration comes to mind just as the trees start to rustle once again, or the sun finally breaks through a brooding cloud.
- Notice how your thoughts align with the natural rhythms of our planet.
- Allow any thought or feeling to move through you naturally.
- When you have finished your reflection, realign your energy once more with the world around you, becoming aware that your feet are firmly anchored to the soil.
- Offer your gratitude, and once more reflect on how you are feeling now compared to when you began your reflection.

The Key to all heartache,
Is to remember who you are

MELTING POT

Looking back over my shoulder,
I can see clearly now...

Space is a melting pot;

An ineffable silence,

in which Universes,

And Universes within Universes

are created,
Only to fade back into the Formless
Before finding expression once again.

A release of what was:
A coming of age of what is.

Honour what is.
The relationship you have with your loved ones in Spirit
continues to evolve.

Having lost my Dad as an infant,
I greet him now,
not just as my Father,
but as the beautiful Soul who gave me life,
and sacrificed his own, far too soon.

I greet him now as a wife and mother in my own right.
I greet him as the grandfather of my two sons,
and
great grandfather to my own grandchildren.

I acknowledge his ongoing Presence in my life with deep
gratitude,knowing we continue to walk together in the
eternal moment.

DARK DUSTY BOXES

Looking back over my shoulder,

I can see clearly now...

that it's important not to struggle for meaning

gleaned from dark, dusty boxes

dumped in some dark corner of the mind!

But to live life's magic,

Moment by moment,

Celebrating its innate wisdom,

From the bottom of my heart.

You are a Star in your own right.
The Earth is your Mother
And
The Sky, your Father

SWEET MOTHER

Looking back over my shoulder,
I can see clearly now...

Winter came much too soon in my young life,
Kicking both Spring,
And
Then Summer into touch.

I spent much of my young childhood on the side-lines,
Watching warring tribes congregating,
Conniving: Jockeying for position,
Stomping all over my field:
My field of dreams.

Looking back over my shoulder,
I can see clearly now...

How much I still wriggle and squirm
To avoid Winter's dark magic
When we approach her Season once again.

True expression is
To be found in the Silence

How can I surrender my grieving heart?

To your cold icy tentacles?

How can I trust you, sweet Mother,

To cut away the dead wood,

Suffocating my dreams?

The gentlest of breezes
Opens the doorway to infinite possibility

CONVERSATIONS WITH THE BREEZE

Looking back over my shoulder
I can see clearly now...

I met the breeze the other day.

She stopped me dead in my tracks,

And, taking my breath away
Told me I'd brought into the Olde World Order.

She sent me packing,
Gently, but firmly in the other direction,

A 180-degree turnabout, back towards the Light,

And, away from frozen wastelands
Where the air lifts me high above menace and pollution.

Where my thoughts are pitch-perfect clear
And where my inspirations are all my own.

Home,
She tells me that's where I'm needed...
Urgently.

We are born into the world
On Wings of Love
Then come down to Earth
With a huge bump,
Forgetting how effortless flight is.

THE AH-HA MOMENT

Looking back over my shoulder,

I can see clearly now...

that sharp intake of breath?

You know the one?

The breath that comes unbidden,

When we step into a world,

Adorned with life, texture, pattern, brilliance,

Rather than dull, plastic uniformity.

The One which comes unbidden

And is an invitation

To take us out of ourselves,

To return us to Self.

The one that comes in an Ah-ha moment

When we can still smell the roses

Despite the rain.

*It's much easier to clear our heads
in the great outdoors,
where landscapes curve naturally
into mountains, valleys and streams,
before
soaring skywards once again*

REMEMBRANCE DAY

Looking back over my shoulder
I can see clearly now...

How even the Silence

Had become chock full

With meaningless noise.

Whilst our broken hearts were left to grieve

For that which we really are,

And the way things were,
or
could have been.

I can see clearly now...

That even the emptiest of Spaces

Still pulse with life's potential

And words yet to be spoken.

Which, nonetheless, need to be spoken,

Before they are misunderstood

And our voices silenced forever:

Our sacrifices all in vain.

Looking back is not to wallow,
but to pick up the golden thread
you have been weaving
throughout the infinity of time.

TABLES

Looking back over my shoulder
I can clearly see now...

The moment of self-realisation,
When my grieving heart was burst wide open

And finally,
I could see.

Where once I felt abandoned,

And isolated,
A table overflowing with Abundance

Had already been set for me.

Healing is...
Cutting the ties to negative thinking,
And
Reopening your Heart
to Love

WORDS

Looking back over my shoulder

I can see clearly now...

That

sometimes words just don't cut the mustard.

There's nothing left to say,

And

Nowhere left to go

Other than within,

Because the space

We once shared together

is empty

And
Ready to move on.

When I learned how important it is
to
live every step of the journey,
I found the rainbow had always been
at my feet.

LIGHT OF HOPE

Looking back over my shoulder

I can see clearly now...

That

The fearsome crack breaking

Each human heart wide open

Is filled to overflowing:

A dam waiting to burst

With unconditional love,

As well as Rainbows

Inviting us to catch

The next light-filled wave
Home.

I love the way mountains stand proud and tall,
no matter which season covers them.

A CALL TO LIFE

Looking back over my shoulder
I can see clearly now...

Just how important reflection is,
Even when our weary mechanistic world
Pushes our buttons so hard,
We're willing to scuttle back
To those dark, dismal treadmills.
You know,
The ones we call life.

*Words make no sense
Unless you're willing to explore
the wide-open spaces
in between!*

AUTUMN'S DEEP YAWNING

Looking back over my shoulder
I can see clearly now...

That action and inaction are close companions.
Inaction, I've discovered, isn't an inertia,
But a surrender to
Life's tsunami-like peaks and troughs,
And the creative wave moving ecstatically through us.
Great Mystery speaks from
The potency of that Silence.
Her message is simple:

' Trust The Miracle of Life's unfolding.'
And, since miracles are simply beyond words,
I just need to acknowledge
That the inspiration rising up

From such a deep space inside me,

is indeed a place of deep integrity,

I am one

with the

Breathe of Life.

Beyond my earthly imaginings.

Autumn is the Season,

Where Silence screams

Louder than any petty command.

Our feelings are designed to make their Presence felt

In the ever lengthening gap between night and day,

And only then poured onto any page,

Where they can find true expression

As riots of colour, shape and innocence.

In celebration of

Life's rich tapestry.

I open my heart To the Miracle of Life

AUTUMN'S RICH PALETTE

Looking back over my shoulder,
I can see clearly now...

How important it is
to live in the Light of Love,
Celebrating its many shades of brilliance,
Rather than diving into a world ravaged by illusion.
I've come to realise
That the darkest tones of life's palette

Deserve a special place
At our Autumnal table too,
Since this is the season of surrender
To the Earth Mother whose oft feared,
all consuming, darkness,
Is a part of that self-same light too.

*Life's full of messy squiggles,
I'm learning to embrace them
rather than iron them out.*

TENDING THE HEARTH

Looking back over my shoulder
I can see clearly now...

As Autumn's passion sweeps the countryside,
I'm home tending the hearth:
Honouring the Sacred Flame
As Women of Olde
Call me to do from beyond the veil.

Keeping it ablaze

Stoking its fire with Summer's once boasting fruits,
Watching them dissolve into mysterious embers
In preparation for Spring's glory.

*True healing
comes from the Soul.
It's not just a smoothing over of physical cracks,
But
a blending of
and
Reconnection to
Body, Mind and Soul.*

WALK IN THE FOREST

Looking back over my shoulder,
I can see clearly now...

How I've taken my time
Getting to know And trust Mother Nature,
As she has getting to know and trust me
With her secrets.

As the wheel turns to face another season
And the breeze moves along with it
She's inviting me
To dive into her magic once again.

She's inviting me

To close my earthly eyes:

To shift both, shape and thought

So I can slip through
Another of her tiny mystical doorways,
To explore the infinite wisdom and magic of Life.

I learned to keep
My heart wide open
At the dawning of every bright new day

RAINBOW BRIDGE

Looking back over my shoulder
I can see clearly now...

That Silence Is not a space to be filled with empty words,
But a place of Surrender
To Life's Mystery
And
Infinite visions waiting to Unfurl.

It's a rainbow bridge, or coat of many colours.
A place of marvel where we pause

Catch our breath, open our hearts

Then turn our faces towards the Sun,
And fly.

Even the darkest day surrenders to the Light

THE KEY TO LIFE

Looking back over my shoulder,

I can see clearly now...

There are not just two sides

To the Coin of Life,

But three!

There is life

As well as death.

But there is also

A shimmering rainbow bridge in between,

And,

I am all three.

*I am at One
with the Breath of Life.*

ROAR

Looking back over my shoulder
I can see clearly now...

It's all been about the Roar:
The 'back-off' roar;
The 'celebratory' roar;
The 'don't mess with me roar',
But most of all the roar
proclaiming you've made it back home,

Centre-stage...
It's your life after all.
The spotlights back on you.
No matter how small
Or insignificant we think we are,

We're all born to Roar.

Live Lovingly
Not fearfully

THE ALCHEMIST

Looking back over my shoulder,

I can see clearly now...

In the Silence,

there is only Love

And

Father Sun, the Alchemist

Whose warmth and compassion transform night-time

struggles into bright new day.

Somewhere on our planet,

Life moves forward basking in his Light.

Whilst elsewhere,

Others are deep in slumber,

Waiting for the Sun's call to rise.

In the Silence,

We are One with all things,

Warmed by Father Sun's Light

And, as the wheel turns, we too move in perfect
symmetry.

It's time to get up and out,
Father Sun's bidding me
To reconnect to his warmth,
As he melts my frozen heart.

CAULDRON

Looking back over my shoulder,
I can see clearly now,...

Silence has a rhythm all of its own,
An infinite wisdom,
A cauldron ablaze with words, yet to be spoken.
Words cannot be forced until their Presence
are truly felt in our hearts.

True Silence is not forbidding or punitive,
It's not a construct born out of heady disconnect.

It does not seek to close you down,
Or to squeeze you into submission
But to ignite your passion for life and living.

My heart was always an open book,
Until you told me I couldn't fly!

I AM AS I AM

Looking back over my shoulder,

I can see clearly now...

That all things are born through an open heart,

And razor-sharp mind,

As yet untrammelled by any desire,

Other than to shake themselves free

From the harsh barren soil

Where no joy could be found

To answer nature's call to roam wild and free,

Just celebrating exactly who

They were meant to be.

When you truly embrace your Passion
You truly embrace life
In all her guises.

ON PAIN AND PERCEPTION

Looking back over my shoulder,
I can see clearly now...

Pain is a perception,
How you see, and more importantly,
experience your letting go
When you surrender to the process of life.

Everything you see around you is a gift,
Absolutely everything.
Even the darkest words,
Or perceived slings and arrows
Hurled across your doorway are merely perceptions
And not the reality of any situation.

The reality is, everything has its foundation in love.
The relationship you have with yourself
Has therefore many layers.
As you ruminate, you will find each layer
Is based on the self same thing, unconditional love.
It has a flavour all its own

So going back is not to wallow,

But to retrieve another thread

Of the tapestry

We've been threading together over time

Based on its energetic signature.

As you chew things over, you'll see

That loves light is the fuel enabling you

To shine light into the darkest places.

In your search

Even the smallest pebble has its place,

Since it hosts Universes within Universes.

Remember you are not insignificant in the eyes of the

Universe:

But you do make waves,

Some tiny, others of tsunami like proportions,

But positively none without significance.

Your responsibility is how you see yourself

When you do make waves.

You are never a nuisance,

Because as a wave you are destined to move,

And that movement quite naturally

Releases energy.

That is your birth right.

If your intention is merely to be

Stars have no doubt

They deserve to be in the spotlight.

Why do you.

Then there should be no sense of

Judgement or recriminations,

Only a celebration

That finally you have given yourself

The joyous space to be a light wave

And a force for good.

The Wisdom Within

The Wisdom Within is a series of poems inspired by Gillian Hollands Lockdown Experience. This is her first poetry pamphlet.

As an experienced Spiritualist Medium, with a background in psychology she hopes these words will help other people come to terms with their own losses.

She's taught meditation and visualisation both online and in live classes for over 15 years, and is a featured writer in Sue Williams anthology, 'Believe you can succeed at 50 plus. '

"*The Wisdom Within illustrates how mindful walks in nature can unleash emotional healing through creative expression and the power of poetry. These evocative poems bring hope and reassurance to others grappling with the ebb and flow of grief and loss*".

Sue Williams, author of 'I am Unique'

Printed in Great Britain
by Amazon